WORSHIP
THROUGH THE
SEASONS
Ideas for Celebration

by Mary Isabelle Hock

Resource Publications, Inc.
San Jose, California 95112

Editorial Director: Kenneth Guentert
Typesetting, illustrations, and design: Ben Lizardi

ISBN: 0-89390-104-0
Library of Congress Catalog Card Number: 86-43231

5 4 3 2

Worship Through The Seasons
Table of Contents

O come, let us worship and bow down, let us kneel before the Lord, our Maker! For He is our God and we are the people that He shepherds.

Psalm 95:6,7

I am the vine, you are the branches. Whoever abides in me, and I in him will bear much fruit, for without Me you can do nothing.

John 15:5

ADVENT
CHRISTMAS
EPIPHANY

Prince Of Peace
Choral Reading

Announcer:	Hear now the words of the prophet Isaiah.
Girls:	The people who were walking in darkness have seen a great light;
Boys:	Those who were living in deep shadows, on them a light has dawned.
Girls:	For to us a child is born,
Boys:	To us a son is given;
All:	And the government will be upon his shoulder.
Girls:	And his name will be called
Voice 1:	Wonderful Counselor,
Voice 2:	Mighty God,
Voice 3:	Everlasting Father,
All:	Prince of Peace.
Girls:	Of the increase of his government and of peace
Boys:	There will be no end.
Girls:	Upon the throne of David,
Boys:	And over his kingdom,
Voice 1:	Establishing it
Voice 2:	Upholding it
Voice 3:	With justice and righteousness
Girls:	From this time forth
Boys:	And for evermore.
All:	The zeal of the Lord of Hosts shall do this.

Isaiah 9:2,6,7

O Come, O Come, Emmanuel
For Movement Choir

Song

O come, O come,	*On knees, head bowed, knuckles of hands on the floor on each side of the body, fingers pointing backward. Drag hands forward slowly, bringing hands up, palms still down.*
Emmanuel.	*Bring arms up high with palms up, face uplifted.*
And ransom captive Israel.	*Right arm moves downward behind body. Left arm moves down and back. Wrists are together, so hands appear like tied hands of prisoner.*
That mourns in lonely exile here	*Head bows low to floor.*
Until the Son of God appear.	*Head comes up slowly. Arms come to front and move up slightly with palms up.*
Rejoice!	*Bring torso and arms up quickly, right knee is on the floor, place left foot on the floor.*
Rejoice!	*Stand! Throw arms up!*
Emmanuel	*Arms lower, extend out in horizontal position.*
Shall come to thee,	*Bring arms in, hands 8" apart, palms up.*
O Israel.	*Arms sweep back, head and torso bow slightly, right foot steps backward.*

Lighting The Advent Candles
The First Sunday

Reader 1:   This is the first Sunday in Advent when we read again of the prophecy and hope of the coming of Christ. It is the time for us to prepare ourselves in spirit, soul, and body for his coming.

Reader 2:   Isaiah 9:6,7

Song: O come, O come Emmanuel
And ransom captive Israel.
That mourns in lonely exile here
Until the Son of God appear.
Rejoice! Rejoice! Emmanuel
Shall come to thee, O Israel!

Reader 3:   Luke 1:26-35

Reader 4:   I light the first candle of the Advent wreath for prophecy and hope.

Song: We light the candle one for prophecy
That Christ will come and set his people free.
We wait with love and longing here
Until the Son of God appear.
Rejoice! Rejoice! Emmanuel
Shall come to thee, O Israel!

Reader 5:   I Thessalonians 5:23

Prayer: Dear Father, we thank You for the prophecy of the coming of Christ, and the hope it has brought to the world. Father, in this Advent season we pray we will truly be ready to receive Him when He comes. Amen.

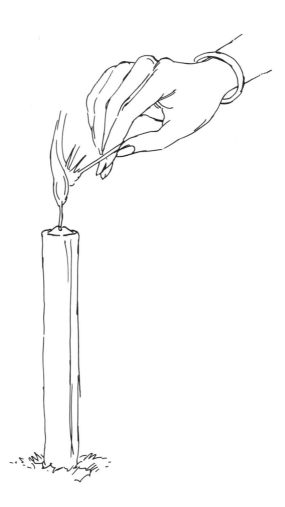

Lighting The Advent Candles
The Second Sunday

Reader 1: This is the second Sunday in Advent when we think of Bethlehem and peace. The prophet Micah in the Old Testament foretold that the birthplace of Jesus was to be in Bethlehem.

Reader 2: In the New Testament the second chapter of Matthew states that when Herod inquired where Christ was to be born, the wise men referred him to the prophecy which reads: "Bethlehem in the land of Judah, you are far from least in the eyes of the rulers of Judah, for out of you shall come a leader to be the shepherd of my people Israel."

(Matt. 2:6 NEB)

Reader 3: As we light the candles of the Advent wreath, let us remember Jesus' birth in Bethlehem and the wondrous peace He has brought to his people.

(Someone lights a candle as each verse is sung.)

Song: We light the candle one for prophecy
That Christ will come and set his people free.
We wait with love and longing here
Until the Son of God appear.
Rejoice! Rejoice! Emmanuel
Shall come to thee, O Israel!

We light the candle two for Bethlehem
Where Christ was born, the sacrificial lamb.
We wait with love and longing here
Until the Son of God appear.
Rejoice! Rejoice! Emmanuel
Shall come to thee, O Israel!

Prayer: Father, we praise You for the birth of Jesus in Bethlehem, and thank You for the peace He has brought his people. And Lord, we pray for your wondrous peace for all people, every where. Amen.

Lighting The Advent Candles
The Third Sunday

Reader 1:   This is the third Sunday in Advent when we think of shepherds and love.

Reader 2:   Luke 2:8-20

Reader 3:   As we light the candles of the Advent wreath let us think of the shepherds glorifying and praising God for his great gift of love for all people.

Song: We light the candle one for prophecy
That Christ will come and set his people free.
We wait with love and longing here
Until the Son of God appear.
Rejoice! Rejoice! Emmanuel
Shall come to thee, O Israel!

We light the candle two for Bethlehem
Where Christ was born the sacrificial lamb.
We wait with love and longing here
Until the Son of God appear.
Rejoice! Rejoice! Emmanuel
Shall come to thee, O Israel!

We light the candle three for shepherds and
love
With praise to God for his great gift from
above.
We wait with love and longing here
Until the Son of God appear.
Rejoice! Rejoice! Emmanuel
Shall come to thee, O Israel!

Prayer: Father, we glorify and praise You too as the shepherds did. Father, we thank You for your wonderful priceless gift of love — Jesus. Amen.

Lighting The Advent Candles
The Fourth Sunday

Reader 1:   This is the fourth Sunday in Advent when we
remember angels and joy.

Reader 2:   Luke 2:10-14

Reader 3:   As we light the candles of the Advent wreath
let us too be filled with great joy just as the
angels were when they proclaimed the good
news of the Christ Child's birth.

Song: We light the candle one for prophecy
That Christ will come and set his people free.
We wait with love and longing here
Until the Son of God appear.
Rejoice! Rejoice! Emmanuel
Shall come to thee, O Israel!

We light the candle two for Bethlehem
Where Christ was born the sacrificial lamb.
We wait with love and longing here
Until the Son of God appear.
Rejoice! Rejoice! Emmanuel
Shall come to thee, O Israel!

We light the candle three for shepherds and
love
With praise to God for his great gift from
above.
We wait with love and longing here
Until the Son of God appear.
Rejoice! Rejoice! Emmanuel
Shall come to thee, O Israel!

We light the candle four for angel's joy
As they told the news of the blessed baby boy.
We wait with love and longing here
Until the Son of God appear.
Rejoice! Rejoice! Emmanuel
Shall come to thee, O Israel!

Litany-Prayer: For the prophecy of the coming of Christ and
the hope that it has brought into the world

WE THANK YOU, FATHER.

For Jesus' birth in Bethlehem and the
wondrous peace He has brought to his people

WE THANK YOU, FATHER.

For the shepherds glorifying and praising God
for his great gift of love for all people

WE THANK YOU, FATHER.

For the angels singing with joy the good news
of the Christ child's birth

WE THANK YOU, FATHER, AMEN.

Christmas Eve Candlelight Service

ORGAN PRELUDE

INTROIT   *(Spoken)*   Charles Wesley

Choir: Hail the heaven-born prince of peace!
Hail the sun of righteousness!
Light and life to all He brings
Risen with healing in his wings.

Cong.:   GLORY TO GOD IN THE HIGHEST
AND ON EARTH, PEACE, PEACE.

Choir: Mild He lays his glory by,
Born that man no more may die;
Born to raise the sons of earth,
Born to give them second birth.

Cong.:   GLORY TO GOD IN THE HIGHEST
AND ON EARTH, PEACE, PEACE.

Carol: "Joy to the World"

LIGHTING OF ADVENT WREATH

Prayer: Father, in this Advent season we have been
preparing ourselves in spirit, soul, and body
for the coming of Christ. Father, we pray that
we are truly ready to receive Him in our hearts.
Amen.

Reader: Let us again light the four candles of the
Advent wreath to commemorate the
miraculous birth of Jesus in Bethlehem, and
then as we light the white candle for Christ, our
Lord, let us invite Him to be born again in us.

SONG: We light the candle white for Christ, our king.
For love and joy and peace that He does bring.
Be welcome in our hearts, Lord, we pray.
Be our true light and life to guide our way.
Rejoice! Rejoice! Emmanuel
Has come to thee, O Israel!

SILENT PRAYER AND REFLECTION

CAROL: "O Little Town of Bethlehem"

ANTHEM

OFFERING

SCRIPTURE: John 1:1-5, 9

CHRISTMAS MEDITATION

CAROL: "Angels from the Realms of Glory"
(While lighting candles in congregation)

CAROL: "Silent Night"
*(All raise and lower candles as pastor raises
and lowers his candle. Extinguish candles
before departure.)*

Children's Christmas Pageant

Narrator: Now it came to pass in those days that a decree went forth from Caesar Augustus that a census of the whole world should be taken. This first census took place while Quirinius was governor of Syria and everyone went to his own town to register.

So Joseph also went up from the town of Nazareth in Galilee to Judea, to Bethlehem the town of David, because he belonged to the house and line of David. He went there to register with Mary, who was pledged to be married to him and was expecting a child.

Hymn: "O Little Town of Bethlehem" *(2 verses)*

(Mary and Joseph enter)

Narrator: And it came to pass while they were there, that the days for her to be delivered were fulfilled. And she brought forth her first-born son, and wrapped Him in swaddling clothes, and laid Him in a manger, because there was no room for them in the inn.

Violin Solo: "O Holy Night"

(Angel brings in infant, shows Him to all the congregation and places Him in crib. Other angels join in dance, then go off.)

Narrator: And there were shepherds in the same district living in the fields and keeping watch over their flock by night.

Hymn: "The First Noel" *(2 verses)*

(Shepherds enter)

(Angel enters)

Narrator: And behold, an angel of the Lord stood by them and the glory of the Lord shone round about them, and they were sore afraid.

Angel: Be not afraid, for behold, I bring you good news of great joy which will be for all people. For to you is born this day in the city of David, a saviour, who is Christ the Lord. And this will be a sign for you; you will find the babe wrapped in swaddling clothes and lying in a manger.

(Other angels enter)

Narrator: And suddenly there was with the angel a multitude of the heavenly host praising God and saying,

Angels: Glory to God in the highest, and on earth peace among men of good will.

Violin Solo: "Hark the Herald Angels Sing"

(Angels dance and pay homage to child)

Narrator: And it came to pass, when the angels had departed from them, that the shepherds were saying to one another, "Let us go over to Bethlehem and see this thing which has come to pass that the Lord has made known to us."

(Shepherds move toward crib and kneel)

So they went with haste, and they found Mary and Joseph and the babe lying in the manger. And when they had seen, they understood what had been told them concerning the child.

Song: "We Three Kings"

(Kings enter singing)

Narrator: Now when Jesus was born in Bethlehem of Judea in the days of Herod the king, behold, wise men from the East came to Jerusalem. And lo, the star which they had seen in the East went before them, till it came to rest over the place where the child was.

When they saw the star, they rejoiced exceedingly with great joy: and going into the house they saw the child with Mary, his mother, and they fell down and worshiped Him. Then opening their treasures, they offered Him gifts, gold, frankincense and myrrh.

Choir: "Away in the Manger"

Choir: "Bring a Torch, Jeanette Isabella"

(One dancer enters, then other dancers as villagers follow. The choir with candles move to the center of the sanctuary. A few villagers and choir help to light the candles in the congregation.)

Hymn: "Silent Night"

(Candles may be raised and lowered during hymn. Candles are blown out before departure.)
(Luke 2: 4,5 NIV; Matt 2: 1,9-11, RSV; Luke 2: 13 RSV)

Dance A Christmas Carol
Here We Come A-caroling

Form two concentric circles, one person from inner circle faces person on outer circle.

Here we come a-caroling
Among the leaves so green.
Here we come a wand'ring
So fair to be seen.

Do-si-do passing on the right.

Do-si-do passing on the left.

Love and joy come to you.
And to you glad Christmas
   too;
And God bless you and send
   you
A Happy New Year,
And God send you a Happy
   New Year!

Grand right and left all around.

Dance A Christmas Carol
God Rest Ye Merry Gentlemen

God rest ye merry gentlemen
Let nothing you dismay,
For Jesus Christ our saviour
Was born upon this day.

All join hands in a circle and moving to the right, starting on the word "rest" take 3 steps, right foot, left, right, and then kick upward with left foot. Then moving to the left, step left, right, left, and kick up with the right foot.
(Repeat sequence.)

To save us all from Satan's
    power
When we were gone astray.

Running to the right with small steps.

Running to the left with small steps.

O tidings of comfort and joy,
Comfort and joy,
O tidings of comfort and joy!

All move to center.
Circle moves back.
Move to center with joined hands held high and lift up on toes on last "joy."

Dance A Christmas Carol
Go Tell it on the Mountain

Refrain:

Go tell it on the mountain
Over the hills and every
  where.
Go tell it on the mountain
That Jesus Christ is born.

*Make two concentric circles of
an equal number of people. The
inner circle goes counter-
clockwise while the outer circle
goes clockwise. Right hands
touch in greeting as circles
move.*

While shepherds kept their
  watching

*Kneel, right knee on floor, left
foot on floor. Right arm sweeps to
the right.*

O'er silent flocks by night.
Behold throughout the
  heavens
There shone a holy light.

*Left arm sweeps to left.
Both arms sweep in together and
go up. Hands up high move
slowly outward.*

Refrain

The shepherds feared and
  trembled
When lo! above the earth
Rang out the angel chorus
That hailed our saviour's
  birth.

*All kneel, right knee on floor, left
foot on floor, while two or three
angels dance and two or more
sing verse.*

Refrain

Down in a lowly manger
The humble Christ was born.
And brought us God's
  salvation
That blessed Christmas morn.

*All kneel in prayerful position
while soloist sings verse. Lift
face and arms heavenward.*

Dance A Christmas Carol
Jingle Bells

All people join hands to make a circle and step rhythmically in place on the verse. Their joined hands raise up to enable the "driver" and passengers to pass under and go in and out of the circle.

Dashing through the snow,

One person chosen as the "driver" steps lightly, jingling sleigh bells and passes under raised arms in and out of the circle.

In a one horse open sleigh,

On "sleigh," driver touches someone to be "number one" who follows him.

O'er the fields we go,
Laughing all the way.

On "way," "number one" chooses "number two" to follow in line.

Bells on bob-tail ring,
Making spirits bright,

On "bright," "number two" chooses "number three" to follow in line.

What fun it is to ride and sing
A sleighing song tonight.

By the word "tonight," the driver and passengers get back into the circle.

Chorus:

Jingle bells, jingle bells,	*All in circle step joyfully to the left.*
Jingle all the way!	*On "way," all joined hands stretch up high.*
Oh what fun it is to ride	*Arms down, hands still joined, everyone steps joyfully to the right.*
In a one-horse open sleigh!	*On "sleigh," all arms raise high.*
	(Repeat sequence)
Verse two	*"Driver" hands bells to "number three" who is now the new driver.*

An Epiphany Celebration

Gather the congregation together in an area near the sanctuary to explain the service. Ask each person to write a favorite Bible verse that has blessed him or her on the paper provided. Collect the scriptures and put them in offertory baskets to be used later in the service.

Explain how the three kings will be chosen and that at the end of the service all will follow them out doing the tripudium step while singing the chorus of "Go Tell It on the Mountain."

Practice one verse only of the processional hymn and the tripudium step which early Christians used for processionals. Tripudium means "three steps" which is a repetition of three steps forward and one back. Several people abreast (check width of aisles) link arms row after row and process. The verse- speaking choir can lead the way and take their place at the front of the sanctuary. Keep singing the first verse and chorus until all persons are seated.

Processional: "We've A Story to Tell to the Nations"

Choir: Listen to the prophet Isaiah!
Do listen well! Hear him foretell
Of the men from afar
Who followed a star
Bringing incense and gold
As the child they behold,
And proclaiming the praise of the Lord.

(Isaiah steps forward from choir)

Isaiah: Arise, shine, for your light has come.
And the glory of the Lord rises upon you.

See, darkness covers the earth
And thick darkness is over the peoples.
But the Lord rises upon you
And his glory appears over you.
Nations will come to your light,
And kings to the brightness of your dawn.

Lift up your eyes and look about you.
All assemble and come to you;
Your sons come from afar,
And your daughters are carried on the arm.

Then you will look and be radiant,
Your heart will throb and swell with joy.
The wealth on the seas will be brought to you.

To you the riches of the nations will come.
Herds of camels will cover your land.
Young camels of Midian and Ephah.
And all from Sheba will come,
Bearing gold and incense
And proclaiming the praise of the Lord.

(Isaiah 60:1-6NIV)

(Isaiah steps back with choir)

Hymn: "O Come, O Come, Emmanuel" *(1 verse)*

(Congregation sing and movement choir dance)

Choir: God sent his angel, Gabriel
To Nazareth in Galilee
With a message for Mary, already betrothed

To Joseph, the bridegroom to be.

(Gabriel and Mary step forward from choir)

Gabriel:	Hail, O favored one. The Lord is with you! Do not be afraid, Mary, You have found favor with God.

Behold! you will conceive in your womb
And bring forth a son
And shall call his name JESUS.

He will be great
And will be called the Son of the Most High
And the Lord God will give to Him
The throne of his father David.
He will reign over the house of Jacob
     forever;
And of his kingdom there will be no end.

Mary: How can this be, for I have no husband?

Gabriel: The Holy Spirit will come upon you
And the power of the Most High will
     overshadow you.
Therefore, the child to be born will be called
     holy,
The son of God.

Mary: Behold, I am the handmaiden of the Lord.
Let it be to me according to your word.

(Gabriel steps back with the choir)

Mary:	My soul magnifies the Lord.
	And my spirit rejoices in God my saviour.
	For He has regarded the low estate of his handmaiden.
	For behold, henceforth all generations will call me blessed;
	For He who is mighty has done great things for me.
	Holy is his name.
	And his mercy is on those who fear Him
	From generation to generation.
	<div align="right">(Luke 1:28, 30-35, 38, 46-50 RSV)</div>
	(Mary, Joseph and child can make a tableau while congregation sings.)
Hymn:	"O Little Town of Bethlehem" *(1 verse)*
Choir:	In Bethlehem Town all inns were filled;
	Joseph sought for a place to stay.
	Mary gave birth to her first-born son
	And laid Him in a stall of fresh sweet hay.
	All who saw the holy child
	Were blessed by his radiant light.
	May you too receive a blessing
	As you read God's word with fresh insight.
Gabriel:	We are waiting for the three wise men who are seeking the radiant light of the Christ child. As we sing the next hymn, please stand if your blessing indicates you are one of the kings. We will go with you to pay homage to the child.
Hymn:	"Good Christian Men Rejoice" *(3 verses)*

(Choir goes through aisles bearing baskets of blessings and names of three kings. All select a blessing and the three kings stand. Mary, Joseph, and 2-year-old child stand in front of sanctuary.)

Hymn: "We Three Kings"

(Everyone sings verse 1 and chorus as Gabriel and three kings go forward. Balthasar reads verse 2, kneels, and presents gift. Melchior reads verse 3, kneels, and presents gift; Caspar reads verse 4, kneels, presents gift. Kings remain kneeling while congregation sings verse 5 and chorus.)

Gabriel: O blessed child, the kings have followed your radiant light to worship you and bring you gifts. May we all see the radiant light of Christ that we too can worship Him and bring Him gifts. Let us go forth into the world spreading his light and proclaiming the truth of the gospel of Jesus Christ, our Lord.

Hymn: "Go Tell It on the Mountain"

(Gabriel, Joseph, Mary, child, and three kings lead out followed by all doing the tripudium step. Keep repeating the chorus until all assemble around the wassail bowl and cookies.)

More carols may be sung, old Christmas trees burned, or carols may be danced for other Epiphany celebration activities.

LENT
EASTER

Psalm 130
For Movement Choir

From the depths I call to You, Yahweh.	*On knees, head slightly bowed, hands in front, one above the other with palms up, near the floor in angular tense position. Bring hands slowly up, fingers apart.*
Lord, listen to my cry for help!	*Arms and head move upward.*
Listen compassionately to my pleading.	*Move arms slightly for emphasis.*
If You never overlooked our sins.	*Bring hands downward to chest level, palms up, a few inches apart.*
Lord, how could anyone survive?	*Extend arms out horizontally.*
But You do forgive us.	*Still on knees, bring torso up, clench fists in front.*
And for that we love and praise You.	*Cross arms in front, lift arms to praise position.*
I wait for You, Yahweh.	*Face still uplifted, bring arms slowly downward.*
My soul waits for You. I rely on your promises. My soul relies on You, Yahweh.	*Continue bringing arms down. Still on knees, bring torso down. Hands near floor sweep upward, inward, out. Face uplifted.*
For it is with You That mercy is to be found,	*Arms move from out to in, palms up, together.*
And a generous redemption:	*Arms sweep out horizontally.*
It is You who redeems us From all our sins.	*Arms come together palms up, head bows down, hands on each side move down and back.*

Adapted from Jerusalem Bible

Ash Wednesday

PRELUDE

CALL TO WORSHIP: Ps. 32:1-3, 5; 130:7 NIV
Blessed is he whose transgressions are forgiven
Whose sin is covered.
Blessed is the man whose sin the Lord
Does not count against him,
And in whose spirit there is no deceit.
WHEN I KEPT SILENT, MY BODY WASTED AWAY
THROUGH MY GROANING ALL DAY LONG
I ACKNOWLEDGED MY SIN TO YOU, LORD,
AND YOU FORGAVE THE GUILT OF MY SIN.
Put your hope in the Lord!
For with the Lord is unfailing love,
And with Him is full redemption.

HYMN: "Amazing Grace"

PRAYER OF CONFESSION: OUR FATHER, YOU SENT
JESUS TO SAVE THOSE WHO ARE LOST. JUDGE US
WITH LOVE AND LIFT THE BURDEN OF OUR
SINS. HAVE MERCY, O GOD, AND FORGIVE US
OUR SINS IN THE NAME OF JESUS CHRIST, YOUR
SON, OUR SAVIOUR. AMEN.

FIRST LESSON: Joel 2:12-19

ACT OF PRAISE: "Gloria Patri"

SECOND LESSON: II Corinthians 5:20b-6:2

ANTHEM: Choir

GOSPEL LESSON: Matthew 6:1-6, 16-21

**INVITATION TO THE OBSERVANCE OF LENTEN
DISCIPLINE**

SILENT EXAMINATION OF CONSCIENCE: *On the small piece of paper in this bulletin write a particular sin or characteristic in your life which is hurtful or unjust to others or yourself. These will be brought by each person in procession and placed upon a grate to be burned with palm branches for ashes.*

SOLO: "O Lamb of God"

PROCESSION OF CONFESSION AND INCINERATION

PRAYER OVER ASHES: Merciful Father, hear us your children, as we come before You acknowledging the sin in our lives. Lord, we humbly ask your forgiveness. We thank You for your promise, Lord, that if we confess our sins, You are faithful and just and will forgive our sins, and purify us from all unrighteousness. We thank You for your mercy and grace, and for your great love. In the name of Jesus Christ, our Lord and saviour, Amen.

IMPOSITION OF ASHES: *Worshipers in each section will come forward and then return to their seats by the opposite end of the row. Bring your offering with you and leave it in the offering plates on the small table. The choir will come first and then return to lead in singing until all have received.*

HYMN: "Come Ye Disconsolate"

HYMN: "The Lord is My Shepherd"

ABSOLUTION: In the name of Jesus Christ you are forgiven. IN THE NAME OF JESUS CHRIST WE ARE FORGIVEN.

PRAYER:

HYMN: "Lord, Dismiss Us with Thy Blessing"

BENEDICTION

Father Most Holy
Song

Father, most holy,
Lord of all creation,
Hear my supplication.
Father, O Father, hear my plea.
Forgive all my transgressions,
Cleanse and purify me.
Lord, fill me with love, compassion,
mercy and thy truth.

Father, most holy,
Father, almighty,
Have mercy.
Lord, redeem thy servant,
Lord, grant me thy pardon.
Lord, fill me with Christ,
Let me love and serve Thee
Throughout all eternity.

Father, most holy,
Father, almighty,
Redeem me.
Lord, give me thy wisdom.
Lord, grant me thy vision.
Lord, fill me with Christ.
Let me love and serve Thee
Throughout all eternity.
Amen.

Lyrics: Mary Isabelle Hock
Music: "Ave Maria" by Bach-Gounod

Prayer Of Confession
Song

Father in heaven, hear us we pray.
We seek Thee in earnest supplication,
With fervent hearts we do obey.
Tis Thou, tis Thou canst save our souls,
Save our souls from sin.
Father, Father in thy mercy hear us.
Within thy love we'll find repose.
To Thee we humbly ask thy pardon.
Dearest Lord, relieve our worldly woes,
Father, O Father.

Father in heaven, pure and stainless let us be.
Forgive us all our transgressions.
O Father, Father, hear our plea.
Tis Thou, tis Thou canst save our souls,
Save our souls from sin.
Remove, Lord, our every imperfection
By thy grace and loving mercy.
We yield our will to thine forever and ever,
Dearest Lord, we give our lives to Thee.
Father, Amen.

Lyrics: Mary Isabelle Hock
Music: "Ave Maria" by Franz Schubert

A Holy Week Celebration

This is an intergenerational experience for all ages — babes in parents' arms, the young, teen-agers, and adults, singles and families. Prior to the celebration give out parts to people in the congregation that all may search the scriptures to be familiar with the roles. Instruct all to use their own words—ad lib—listen, and react to what other people say. The part of Jesus will require much preparation. It would be wise for Jesus to practice with one segment at a time before the celebration.

Wear modern day casual dress and make the Bible come alive! You may use each of the following segments, omit some, or add some. This is your own real drama of Holy Week, so fit it to your people and to your own surroundings.

1. ROAD TO JERUSALEM (church parking lot)
(Jesus and disciples move toward Jerusalem— the church)

Crowd: *(waving palms)* Hosanna! Hosanna! Blessed is He who comes in the name of the Lord!

2. MONEY CHANGERS IN TEMPLE
(Jesus and others enter temple. Buyers and sellers barter.)

Jesus: *(angry, overturns tables)* This is my Father's house. It is a house of prayer, but you have made it a den of robbers.

Seller 1:   What right have you to do this? You've ruined all our goods!

Seller 2:   Come on, let's get him. We'll make him pay for this.

Jesus:	Destroy this temple and in three days I will raise it up.
Seller 1:	It has taken 46 years to build this temple and you say you'll raise it up in 3 days — you're crazy!
Seller 2:	Come on, let's pick up our stuff. We'll get you for this! *(shakes fist at Jesus)*

3. TEACHING AND HEALING (move into sanctuary)

Blind man *(led by another):*	Lord, Son of David, have mercy on me. I can't see. Please restore my sight.
Jesus:	*(places hands on blind man)* Receive your sight.
Blind man:	I can see! Thank You, Master. Thank You, Master.
Leper:	Jesus, if you are willing, you can make me clean.
Jesus:	*(touching leper)* I am willing. Be clean.
Leper:	*(kneeling)* Thank You, Jesus.
	(Crippled woman limps nearby)
Jesus:	Woman, you are set free from your infirmity. Be healed.

Woman:	*(straightens up)* The Lord be praised. I can walk! It's a miracle.
Nicodemus:	Rabbi, we know you are a teacher from God; for no one can do the miracles you do unless God is with him.
Jesus:	Truly I say to you, unless one is born anew, he cannot see the kingdom of God.
Nicodemus:	How can a man be born when he is old? Can he enter a second time into his mother's womb and be born?
Jesus:	Unless one is born of water and the spirit, he cannot enter the kingdom of God. That which is born of the flesh is flesh, and that which is born of the spirit is spirit. You must be born again.
	(Children start coming to Jesus.)
Peter:	Hey you kids, the Master is busy — get lost!
Jesus:	Let the children come to me and don't stop them, for the kingdom of God belongs to them. Truly I say to you, whoever does not receive the kingdom of God like a child shall not enter it. Bless you, child. Bless you, child.*(Jesus touches and embraces the children.)*
Jesus:	Peter and John, it is time to make preparation for our Passover meal.
John:	Where will you have us prepare it, Jesus?

Jesus:	A man carrying a jar of water will meet you; follow him into the house he enters and ask the owner, "Where is the guest room that I am to eat the Passover with my disciples?" He will show you a large upper room furnished and you can make preparations there.
Peter:	We'll get it all ready, Master.
Jesus:	We will join you soon.
Man:	*(kneeling)* Teacher, what must I do to inherit eternal life?
Jesus:	You know the commandments: do not kill; do not commit adultery; do not steal; honor your father and mother.
Woman:	Of all the commandments, which is the most important?
Jesus:	The most important one is this: Love the Lord your God with all your heart and with all your soul and with all your mind and with all your strength. The second one is this: Love your neighbor as yourself. There are no commandments greater than these.

4. UPPER ROOM (dining area)

Jesus:	Come, all of you! Let us share the Passover meal together. *(All follow Jesus linking arms and singing, "We Are One in the Spirit.")*

Jesus:	Father, we ask you to bless this food and bless all partaking of it. Amen.
All:	Amen. *(dinner conversation)*
Jesus:	One of you, my disciples, will betray me.
Peter:	Surely it is not I.
John:	Surely not me, Lord.
Jesus:	The Son of Man will go just as it is written about Him. But woe to that man who betrays the Son of Man! It would be better for him if he had not been born. (Jesus picks up bread.) Holy Father, bless this thy bread. Amen. This is my body which is given for you. Eat ye of it. *(Each person takes a portion of bread and passes loaf on.)*
Jesus:	Father, bless every drop in this cup for thy eternal glory, Amen. This is my blood of the covenant which is poured out for many for the forgiveness of sin. Drink ye of it. This do in remembrance of me.

(Pass the cup)

(All partake of communion; sing "Let Us Break Bread Together")

(Mark 10:17, 19; 12:30, 31; John 3: 2-7 RSV)

The Twelve Disciples Of Christ
Choral Reading

All:

Jesus sent out 12 disciples
With authority to teach,
To heal, cast out demons,
Cleanse, and to preach.

Solo 1:

There was Simon, called Peter,
And his brother, Andrew,

Solo 2:

And James, son of Zebedee,
With his brother, John.

Solo 3:

There was James, son of Alphaeus,

Solo 4:

Thaddaeus and Thomas too;

Solo 5:

Matthew and Philip,
And Bartholomew.

Solo 6:

There was Simon the zealot,
And who did we miss?

All:

Judas Iscariot
Who betrayed with a kiss.
These were the 12 disciples
With authority to teach,
To heal, cast out demons,
Cleanse, and to preach.

Matthew 10:1-4, 8

Psalm One Hundred
Choral Reading

All:	Make a joyful noise unto the Lord, All ye lands!
Low voices:	Serve the Lord with gladness.
High voices:	Come before his presence with singing!
Low voices:	Know ye that the Lord, He is God!
High voices:	It is He that has made us And not we ourselves.
All:	We are his people And the sheep of his pasture.
Low voices:	Enter into his gates with thanksgiving.
High voices:	And into his courts with praise.
Low voices:	Be thankful unto Him
High voices:	And bless his name.
All:	For the Lord is good! His mercy is everlasting And his truth endures to all generations.

THANKSGIVING:
(Children can wave crepe paper streamers of autumn colors on first and last lines.)

PALM SUNDAY:
(Begin and end with "Hosanna, Hosanna!" as children wave palm branches.)

Palm Sunday
Choral reading

Children wave palm branches in procession

Choir: Hear the multitudes shout and joyously sing,

Children: "Hosanna! Hosanna! Praise to our king!"

Choir: See the happy children skipping and singing, Strewing the garlands of flowers they're bringing.

The disciples rejoice for their Master this day As He rides in triumph with palms in his way.
The throngs press forward with admiration and love;
Expectant with happiness for his kingdom above.

Children: "God bless Jesus, King David's son!
Praise to our Lord for the miracles He's done.
Praise God in highest heaven, our King is here,
Teaching and healing all who come near."

Choir: Raise all your voices to heaven and sing,

Children: "Hosanna! Hosanna! Praise to our king!"

Choir: Raise your voices higher! Let the heavens ring!

Choir and children: "Hosanna! Hosanna! Rejoice! He's our king!"

Carrying The Cross
Movement Choir

Music: "Were You There"

Solo Instrument: Cello, violin, or voice

As the music begins, Christ at the back of the church picks up the heavy imaginary cross, and slowly struggling with it makes his way to the front of the church. Two Roman soldiers whip Him when He stumbles. The soldiers take Christ up on the platform, and turn Him around, so that He is facing the congregation. With Christ standing and the cross behind Him, the two soldiers stretch out Jesus' arms and pound a nail, 1-2-3 in his hands. The agony is expressed on Christ's face and again as the soldiers pound, 1-2-3 nailing his feet. The soldiers stand back, look at Christ in contempt and walk off.

Jesus' friends approach expressing their sorrow. They convey their love to Him, turn and comfort each other, and prayerfully lift their hands to God.

Jesus drops his head in death. The friends react in despair and stand motionless. After a pause, Christ lifts his head and with a serene expression on his face, beckons to his friends to come follow Him. Christ with outstretched hands leads the way as his friends, praising God, joyously follow.

Sorrow At The Cross
Movement

---

1. Choreography for two dancers and violinist (or vocalist) using the music, "Panis Angelicus" by C. Franck.

2. On the introduction of the music one dancer approaches the altar with uplifted hands and in sorrow kneels at the altar. The second dancer comes from a different area, lifts hands to God and then kneels.

3. On the segment of music where the violinist begins his solo, the two dancers rise to their knees, gracefully moving first the right arm to the right and back, and then the left arm to the left and back. The dancers stand upright with supplicating gestures to God. They turn away from the altar not seeing each other. The first dancer goes to the side and stands in prayerful position while the second dancer does a solo. Then the second dancer assumes a prayerful position while the first dancer does a movement solo.

4. On the last segment of the music as the violinist begins after a short interlude, the dancers see each other and share their grief at the betrayal of Jesus. They move to each other, to the altar, they pass by each other to opposite sides with the arm in front extended high and the arm in back on a downward slant. The dancers move back to the altar with faces and arms uplifted to God and then they humbly kneel.

The Crown Of Thorns
Movement Choir

As the seated congregation sings the first verse of "Were You There," nine people slowly process in the center aisle toward the altar. The first person is holding a crown of thorns and the remaining eight are walking in pairs with heads slightly bowed and arms at their sides.

The person with the crown ascends all the steps and, facing the altar, lifts the crown high; and during the second verse, can lower and raise it and do movements similar to the rest of the choir.

The remaining eight also continue to face the altar and take the following positions to form a cross: 2 is on the lower step; 3, 4, and 5 should all be on the same step on a lower level; 6 should be on a lower step; and, depending on the number of steps available, 7, 8, and 9 can be on lower steps so the symbol of the cross is visible. All dancers stand reverently until the end of the first verse.

SECOND VERSE

First line: Dancers raise their hands and arms to the chest level and then out horizontally.

Second line: Bring hands slowly back to the chest and hold in clenched position and then kneel.

Third line: The right hand unfolds and moves to the right and the left hand follows several inches behind.

First tremble: Fingers tremble.

Second tremble: Bring trembling fingers up over head.

Third tremble: Trembling fingers move to the left with left arm several inches ahead of right arm.

Last line: Bring both arms up and cross them on the chest and bow head.

THIRD VERSE: Arms slowly unfold and go to sides. Head goes up and all dancers stand, turn on the right, pause, and slowly and solemnly process out in pairs with heads bowed and arms at the sides.

In Remembrance Of Me

Mary Isabelle Hock

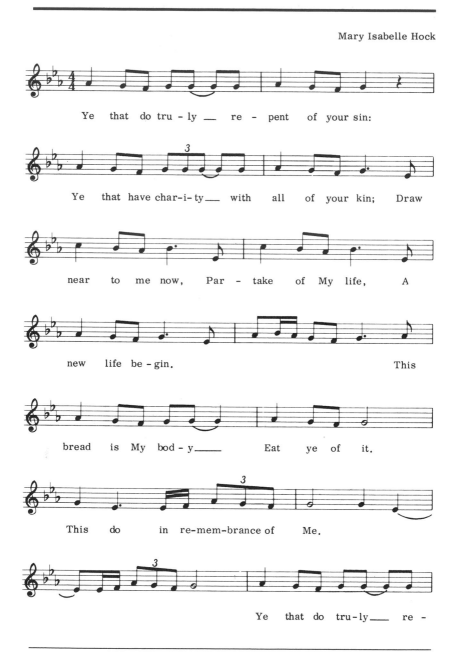

Ye that do tru - ly __ re - pent of your sin:

Ye that have char-i- ty __ with all of your kin; Draw

near to me now, Par - take of My life, A

new life be - gin. This

bread is My bod - y __ Eat ye of it.

This do in re-mem-brance of Me.

Ye that do tru - ly __ re -

pent   of your sin;   Ye   that have char-i-ty____ with

all   of your kin;   Draw   near   to   me   now,   Par-

take   of My life,   A   new   life be-gin.

This   is My blood   of   the

cov-e-nant which is poured   out for man-y____ for the for-give-

ness of sin.   Drink ye of it.   This do   in re-mem-brance of

Me.

Lo!   I am with   you   al - ways.

In Remembrance Of Me
Movement

All movements should be slow and sustained, flowing without stopping, until "the forgiveness of sin" in the song. Love and caring should be conveyed by facial expressions throughout the music.

The vocalist begins with arms gracefully hanging in front in U-shape position with fingers touching and thumbs just above the middle fingers.

SONG	MOVEMENTS
Ye that do truly repent of your sin;	*(thumbs still tucked in) Right palm leads upward and outward (at chest level), then to the right, and then back down to original U position.*
Ye that have charity with all of your kin,	*Left palm leads upward and outward, to the left, and back down to U position.*
Draw near to me now,	*Both hands go outward and slightly up, then come back toward each other as "gathering in."*
Partake of my life,	*Palms going upward very high and slightly outward into a V-shape.*
A new life begin.	*Palms move toward each other, thumbs under fingers. (Visual appearance is a circle.)*
(Interlude)	*Arms arc downward creating a circle.*

This bread is my body.	*As circle is completed, hands come together palms up.*
Eat ye of it.	*Palms go to left, as though serving communion.*
This do in remembrance of Me.	*Palms go back to center front and then right side.*
(Interlude)	*Left palm goes back to left side and both hands return to U position.*
"Ye that do truly" — to "A new life begin."	*Same as above.*
This is my blood of the covenant	*Both arms slowly stretch straight outward in visual symbol of the cross.*
Which is poured out for many for the forgiveness of sin!	*On "sin" arms and fingers have electrical jolt with fingers stretching far apart from each other.*
Drink ye of it. This do in remembrance of Me.	*Hold position.* *Hold position.*
(Interlude)	*Fingers go back together, arms slowly return to U position.*
Lo! I am with you	*Palms up in front, going outward a few inches,*
Always.	*Supplicating hands move a few inches more, stop, and hold.*

Easter Sunrise Service

by Rev. Eugene Bacon

(All persons gather in the pre-dawn darkness)

CRY OF DESPAIR

CALL OF HOPE

PRAYER OF CONFESSION

God, despair does so often fill our lives. The gloom of late winter, the weights of thankless responsibilities, perplexing decisions that admit of no acceptable solutions, even headaches and indigestion leave us depressed. Over and over again we bemoan our fate, and complain to ourselves of life's injustices — as if we were the first and only person confronted by difficulties. Help us, God, to believe again in resurrected living. Help us to work through our sorrows to a deeper joy, and reject despair for abundant life. May we be guided by our resurrected Lord and saviour, Jesus Christ, who conquered not only despair but death itself. In the name of Jesus Christ we pray. Amen.

CHRIST CANDLE IS LIT

CRY OF JOY

"He is risen. Let us follow Him. There is light and life- a-plenty for all." *(Acolytes receive their light from the Christ candle and proceed to light the candles of all the people as they follow the Christ candle in two lines up to the sanctuary. Candles should be blown out before entering the sanctuary.)*

WORDS OF ASSURANCE

"Today, Christ the Lord is truly risen."

HYMN   "Jesus Christ is Risen Today"

OLD TESTAMENT LESSON: Exodus 3:108

ANTHEM

NEW TESTAMENT LESSON: Mark 16:1-8

HYMN: "Good Christian Men, Rejoice and Sing"

DRAMATIC PRESENTATION: Chancel Drama

RESPONDING TO THE WORD

INTRODUCTION TO LOVE FEAST

Leader: Christ indeed rose again and is still with us today, bringing life from ashes; from the waste lands of despair, degradation, and meaninglessness. Through the church, Christ, our living Lord, rescues each of us individually from a tangled wilderness of sin, and brings us to the edge of a new life. This new life is symbolized so well in today's Old Testament lesson by the image of a promised land, flowing with milk and honey.

It is fitting then, on this day of celebration, that we should share together a simple meal — a meal of bread, milk, and honey. For all of us, through the resurrection of Jesus Christ, may taste of the whole world as a place upon which God can, at last, look and see that it is very good. Let us pray.

People: Father God through the transforming power of the risen Christ, bless this bread and this milk. They are the simple foods, reminding us that the "promised" land is reserved for those with the "simplicity" of little children.

Leader: O glorious God, through the power of the risen Christ, bless this honey. It is a rich food; reminding us of the rich, abundant joy that is ours when we are raised with Christ into newness of life.

People: Today, as we re-live the Resurrection of Our Lord and Saviour, Jesus Christ, we remember His words on the night before He died: "I shall not drink again of the fruit of the vine until I drink it new in the Kingdom of God." May it be for us today as if our old sinful selves have died. And may this meal be our first meal in the promised land of God's Kingdom.

SOME WORDS ABOUT GIVING AND RECEIVING

SHARING THE MILK AND HONEY: *People come forward in pairs and take turns feeding each other.*

PRAYER AFTER THE SHARING:
Father, thank You for the possibility of Super Life. For life inspired and filled with the Presense of Your Son, Our Risen Lord. Continually renew us God, for You know how weak we are, and help us to spread the Goodly Contagion of Christ Jesus to those who cry out for it. In the Name of Jesus Christ, The King, we pray, Amen.

HYMN: "Crown Him with Many Crowns"

DISMISSAL
Leader: Filled with the Easter message of hope and nourished by the food of the promised land, go forth now into a hopeless, hungry world as bearers of the gift of life.

People: Let us arise and go with joy.

Leader: Amen.

The Cross

Rev. Eugene Bacon

TAPS

HYMN "Were You There"
(*During hymn, three people carry in a large black
wooden cross and stand at front of sanctuary holding it
up.*)

MEDITATION
Do you know what happened to the cross on
Easter Day? It changed from a symbol of brutality,
torture, fear and death — to a symbol of mercy, forgiveness, redemption, and divine love. Before
Christ, the cross was the swastika of the ancient
world. Today it is found on the bedroom walls of
little children.

The cross you see before you is painted black.
Like the old cross it is a symbol of death and
darkness — the darkness of our own lives when
controlled by sin. In a moment I will ask you to
become imitators of Christ, by transforming the
dark symbol of the worst in each of us, into a
symbol of life, a new commitment, into the
glorious, colorful, living cross of Easter.

PROCESSION TO CROSS OF LIFE
(*While singing "Alleluia" each person selects a pre-
cut colorful picture of a puppy, a flower, a landscape, etc.
and walks to cross; tapes picture on cross.*)

RECESS OUT INTO THE WORLD

(While singing the "Battle Hymn of the Republic," all follow the cross, then form a circle around it with hands joined for the benediction.)

In the beauty of the lilies
Christ was born across the sea.
With a glory in his being
That transfigures you and me.
As He died to make men holy
Let us live to make men free.
Come follow the cross of Christ.

Glory! glory! Hallelujah! *(3 times)*
Come follow the cross of Christ.

Christ The Lord Is Risen Today
Circle Dance

Christ the Lord is risen today   *Body moving to the left, left arm raised high, left palm leading; right arm slanted downward.*

Alleluia   *Arms and hands held high; body rotates around in a complete circle. (pivot in place)*

Sons of men and angels say   *Body moving to the right, right arm raised high, right palm leading; left arm slanted downward.*

Alleluia   *Same as above.*

Raise your joys and triumphs high   *Starting low with hands at the sides, move to center of circle with hands going high.*

Alleluia   *Arms held high, body rotates around in place.*

Sing ye heavens, and earth reply   *Move back from center with hands going down.*

Alleluia   *Arms high, body rotating around in place.*

These movements may be repeated on all verses.
Variation: on verses two and three, one dancer could do a solo with all dancers joining in on lines three and four.

Christic The Lord Is Risen Today
Movement Choir

Dancers with multi-colored 20-inch strips of crepe paper streamers process up and down the aisles of the sanctuary on verses one and two.

On "Christ the Lord is risen today," dancers bring right hands with streamers from lower center front up high and circle right and back down; then bring left hands with streamers from lower center front up high and circle left and back down.

On "Alleluia" both hands with streamers at center front circle up high and then to the sides and back down two times. The dancers can continue to repeat these movements for verses one and two while processing.

On verses three and four dancers can hand out streamers to members of the congregation to wave, that all may celebrate with joy the resurrection of the living Christ.

Our Christ Is Risen

Mary Isabelle Hock

Our Christ is ri - sen, Re - joice and ___
Raise your voice in praise to greet our ___

(1) sing, Al - le - lu this Eas - ter morn - ing.
(2) King,

Al - le - lu, Al - le - lu, Al - le - lu, Al - le -

lu, Al - le - lu this Eas - ter morn - ing.

Our Christ Is Risen
Circle Dance

Our Christ is risen; Rejoice and sing,	*Join hands, step joyously to the left.*
Allelu this Easter morning.	*All move to center; raise arms up high; move back to original circle position with arms coming down.*
Raise your voice in praise to greet our king,	*Step joyfully to the right.*
Allelu this Easter morning.	*Move to center, arms up high, move back with arms coming down.*
Allelu, Allelu,	*Hands still joined, slide two steps left.*
Allelu, Allelu,	*Slide two steps right.*
Allelu this Easter morning.	*Do the same as above or move to center with hands held high and hold position until end of somg.*

PENTECOST
KINGDOMTIDE

Enactment Of Pentecost
Drama

Jean Clarkson

A script for use during worship service.
Costumes optional; can be done in modern dress.

Setting: In front of sanctuary, narrator behind pulpit. Some
action takes place on platform, some below.

Characters:

Asad, a resident of Jerusalem
Silas, a tent maker visiting the city
Peter, a disciple
Members of the crowd, men and women
Apostles and followers, men and women
Narrator

(Narrator enters and stands behind the pulpit.)

Asad: *(Enters from left, crossing toward center as Silas enters
fom right.)* Hail, Silas, what brings you to Jerusalem?

Silas: Greetings, Asad! I have a new line of tents which
were selling well along the coast and hope to find a
good market in the city during the festival.

Asad: I wish you well!

*(Apostles and followers enter from right and stand on
platform, praising God quietly with lifted hands.)*

Silas: What is that noise?

Asad: *(Looking toward apostles)* It comes from that house.
What can it mean?

Narrator: And when the day of Pentecost arrived, all the
believers were gathered together in one place. And suddenly

---

there came a sound from heaven as of a rushing mighty wind, and it filled all the house where they were sitting. And there appeared to them cloven tongues like fire that sat upon each of them. And they were all filled with the Holy Spirit and began to speak with other tongues, as the Spirit gave them utterance.

(Enter crowd from left, standing below platform looking up toward apostles.)

There were Jews living in Jerusalem, religious men who had come from every country in the world. They were all excited, because each one of them heard the believers talking in his own language.

Members of crowd: *(speaking individually)*
    — How is it that we hear, each of us in his own native language?
    — Parthians!
    — Medes!
    — Elamites!
    — Dwellers of Mesopotamia!
    — We're from Judea, Cappadocia
    — From Pontus and Asia
    — From Phrygia and Pamphylia, in Egypt
    — And in the parts of Libya about Cyrene!
    — Strangers of Rome, Jews and proselytes, Cretes and Arabians!
    — We hear them speak in our tongues the wonderful works of God!

Crowd: *(Looking puzzled and speaking all at once)*
What does this mean?
(Others in crowd mocking.)
    — These men are full of new wine!
    — They are drunk!
    — I don't understand.

Peter: *(Turning to the crowd)*

Men of Judea and all who dwell in Jerusalem, let this be known to you, and give ear to my words. These men are not drunk, it is only nine o'clock in the morning, but this is what was spoken by the prophet Joel:
And this is what I will do in the last days,
God says:
I will pour out my Spirit upon all men.
Your sons and your daughters will prophesy;
Your young men will see visions,
 and your old men will dream dreams.
Yes, even on my slaves, both men and women,
I will pour out my Spirit in those days, and they
        will prophesy.
I will perform miracles in the sky above,
And marvels on the earth below,
There will be blood, fire, and thick smoke,
The sun will become dark,
And the moon red as blood,
Before the great and glorious day of the Lord arrives.
And then, whoever calls on the name of the Lord
        will be saved.

Listen to these words, men of Israel! Jesus of Nazareth was a man whose divine mission was clearly shown to you by the miracles, wonders, and signs which God did through Him; you yourselves know this, for it took place here among you.

God, in his own will and knowledge, had already decided that Jesus would be handed over to you; and you killed Him, by letting sinful men nail Him to the cross. But God raised Him from the dead. He set Him free from the pains of death, because it was impossible that death should hold Him prisoner.

God has raised this Jesus from the dead, and we are witnesses to this fact. He has been raised to the right side of God and received from Him the

Holy Spirit, as his father had promised; and what you now see and hear is his gift that He has poured out on us.

Therefore, let all the house of Israel know for sure that it is this Jesus, whom you nailed to the cross, that God has made both Lord and Christ.

(Members of crowd look penitent, some with heads bowed, some with hands outstretched.)

Asad: Men and brethren, what shall we do?

Peter: Repent, and be baptized every one of you in the name of Jesus Christ for the remission of sins, and you will receive God's gift, the Holy Spirit. For God's promise was made to you and your children, and to all who are far away — all whom the Lord our God calls to Himself. Men, save yourselves from this corrupt generation.

(Members of crowd move toward Peter and apostles who minister to them.)

Narrator: Those who accepted Peter's message were baptized, and about three thousand were added to their number that day. They devoted themselves to the apostles' teaching and to the fellowship, to the breaking of bread and to prayer.

Everyone was filled with awe, and many wonders and miraculous signs were done by the apostles. All the believers were together and had everything in common. Selling their possessions and goods, they gave to anyone as he had need.

Everyday they continued to meet as a group in the temple, and they had their meals together in their homes, eating the food with glad and humble hearts, praising God, and enjoying the good will of all the people. And the Lord added to the church daily those who were being saved.

Scripture: Acts chapter 2, omitting verses 25-31, 34, 35.

A Pentecost Experience Today

For part of the worship time on Pentecost Sunday, the choir could sing the anthem "Come, Holy Spirit" by John W. Peterson. At the completion of the anthem the choir director would turn to the congregation and have them join in a repeat of the chorus printed in the bulletin.

While singing the chorus again, the choir members would move to be with the congregation, and on the last chord of the chorus the soft melodic sound of wind chimes could fill the sanctuary. The choir would then begin proclaiming, "Be filled with the Holy Spirit" while giving a hug to persons on the end of each row and also saying, "Pass it on."

If this experience is at the end of the worship service, verses one and four of "They'll know we are Christians by our love" would be appropriate, followed by the benediction.

The Story Of Creation
Drama

God spoke the word,
  "Let there be light!"
    He made the sun for day,
      Twinkling stars and moon for night.

God made fluffy clouds
  Floating up so high;
    Now watch the rain and snowflakes
      Swirling from the sky.

God made rivers and streams
  With waves that dip and leap
    Down mountains through the valleys
      And into the ocean deep.

He created fish and whales
  To go swimming in the sea.
    God made robins and hummingbirds,
      The butterfly and the bee.

God made great big elephants;
  Now see the dancing bear,
    The tall giraffe eating leaves
      And hopping rabbits everywhere!

See beautiful flowers growing,
  The wind blowing the wheat.
    God made bananas and apples,
      H'm, many good things to eat.

Then God made man and woman,
  And precious children too.
    Let's clap our hands to praise our God
      For creating all of you!

The Good Samaritan
Movement

Luke 10:30-37

Follow the leader:
Echo the words...   **Imitate the action...**

In the tenth chapter of   *Hold up ten fingers.*
Luke..., a man asked Jesus,

"Who is my neighbor?"   *Both hands on hips.*

So Jesus told this   *Right hand palm up, right hand*
story...about a Jewish man.   *sweeps from left to right.*

One day I put on my san-   *Put on sandals.*
dals;

I tucked my money bag   *Tuck bag under belt.*
under my belt.

I put on my traveling cloak,   *Put on cloak.*

And started walking from   *Walk in place.*
Jerusalem...to go to Jericho.

Up steep rugged   *Arms and feet in motion as if*
 mountains.   *walking up hill.*

Over winding rocky roads.   *Long step in place.*

Past big boulders and dark   *Palms shielding sides of head.*
caves.

I whistled so I wouldn't be   *Whistle.*
afraid.

But robbers jumped out at   *Pull back.*
me.

They hit me.	*Cringe.*
That's all I remember.	*Head down, arms limp.*
After a while I heard foot-steps.	*Feet trod right, left, right, left, 4 even beats.*
I peeked through my swol-len eyes.	*Squint.*
It was a Jewish priest!	*Fold hands in prayer position.*
"Too bad...how sad..."	*Shake head sadly.*
The priest went on his way.	*Hands in prayer position, feet with 4 even beats, right, left, right, left.*
I hurt. Oh, oh.	*Double up in pain, moan.*
I heard different footsteps.	*Lightly limp, right, left, right, left.*
I peeked through my swol-len eyes.	*Squint.*
It was a Levite who helps the priest.	*Arms folded at chest.*
"Oh, somebody must do something about this."	*Back of hand on forehead.*
The Levite went on his way.	*Arms folded at chest, feet lightly limp, right, left, right, left.*
I hurt. Oh, oh.	*Double up in pain, moan.*

Hee-haw!...Did I hear a donkey?	*Look around.*
"Whoa! Need any help?"	*Pull reins.*
A Samaritan jumped off his donkey.	*Jump.*
He took off his cloak,	*Take off cloak.*
Tore it into bandages;	*Tearing motion.*
Took some wine and oil off the donkey,	*Take two objects.*
Then knelt down.	*Kneel.*
He washed my wounds with the wine...Ouch!	*Washing motion.*
He poured olive oil on my sores...Ah!	*Pour.*
He wrapped bandages on my sores.	*Wrap.*
The Samaritan lifted me up,	*Lift.*
And put me on his donkey.	*Hands going down.*
The Samaritan and I went to an inn.	*Fingers tap rhythm of "clippety-clop" on palm of other hand.*
"Hello! Anybody here?"	*Knock.*
"We need a bed."	*Cup hands around mouth.*
The innkeeper and Samaritan lifted me up	*Lift.*

And carried me to a bed in the inn.	*Carry, put down.*
The Samaritan watched over me all night.	*Right hand to the right, left hand to the left at the same time.*
The next morning	*Yawn and stretch.*
The Samaritan gave two denari...to the innkeeper.	*Take two pieces of money from money bag.*
"If you need more money to care for this man,	*Stretch palm out.*
I'll give it to you on my return trip."	*Stretch other palm out.*
The Samaritan continued on his journey.	*Fingers tap rhythm of "clippety-clop" on palm of other hand.*
"Who is my neighbor?"	*Hands on hips.*
Is it the priest?	*Fold hands in prayer position.*
Is it the Levite?	*Arms folded at chest.*
Is it the Samaritan?	*Tap "clippety-clop" with fingers on palm.*
Which of these three is my neighbor?	*Hold up three fingers.*
The one who shows love and mercy.	*Cross arms on chest.*
Go	*Extend one arm out.*
And do the same!	*On "do" extend the other arm.*

Luke 10:27

Mary Isabelle Hock

You shall love the Lord your God with all your

heart, You shall love Him — with all of your

soul, You shall love Him with all your strength and with

all your mind, and love your neigh - bor as — your - self.

Let Us Worship The Lord
Movement

Follow the leader: Echo the words...	*II Chronicles 29* Imitate the action...
King Hezekiah lived in Jerusalem long ago.	*Left arm makes sweeping motion from right to left.*
He loved God...and wanted to live right.	*Raise arms upward...cross arms on chest.*
He called the priests and Levites to come.	*Beckon with arms.*
So the priests and Levites hurried to hear the king.	*Step in place.*
"We must do 2 special things."	*Hold up 2 fingers.*
"We must cleanse ourselves...and cleanse God's house."	*Both hands point to self...and then go outward.*
"First...we must repent...and be holy for God."	*Hold up 1 finger...both hands point to self.*
"Then, we must clean up God's house."	*Hands move from center front outward.*
"Then we can worship Him in the right way."	*Raise arms upward.*
So the priests and Levites prayed and repented.	*Fold hands, bow heads.*
They dusted God's house.	*Hands move in circular motion.*
They cleaned out cobwebs.	*Arms poking high.*
They cleansed the altar...and all the utensils.	*Scrubbing motion.*

They worked so hard for many weeks.	*Wipe brow 2 times.*
Finally, the temple was ready for worship.	*Sigh, hands at hips.*
King Hezekiah proclaimed to all Jerusalem,	*Right arm extended up.*
"Let us go to the house of the Lord!"	*Same position, move hand up and down emphatically.*
Everyone brought offerings to God.	*Two hands together, palms up.*
The musicians played cymbals...	*Palms scrape back and forth.*
They strummed harps...	*Strum harp.*
They blew trumpets...	*Blow trumpet.*
Everyone bowed their heads...	*Bow heads.*
And prayed to God.	*Fold hands.*
Everyone gave thanks and praise to God.	*Raise hands and arms upwards.*
King Hezekiah and all the people rejoiced!	*Throw arms upward, jump!*
They all sang together,	*Palms up, all sing.*
"Come let us gather to worship the Lord."	*Arms raised high*
Verse 2 "Come let us gather to pray to the Lord."	*Fold hands in front.*
Verse 3 "Come let us gather to clap for the Lord."	*Clap hands.*

Come Let Us Gather

Mary Isabelle Hock

1. Come   let us gath - er _____ to
2. Come   let us gath - er _____ to

wor-ship the Lord, __   Wor-ship the Lord, __ Yes to
pray to the Lord, __   Pray to the Lord, __ Yes to

wor - ship __ the Lord. Come let us gath - er in the
pray to _____ the Lord. Come let us gath - er in the

Pres - ence __ of God to wor - ship Him.
Pres - ence __ of God to pray to Him.

Verse 3   To clap for the Lord

Luke 4:1-13
Drama For Verse-Speaking Choir

The choir stands still, while Jesus and the devil use appropriate movements to dramatize the words (from the Good News Bible).

Choir: Jesus returned from the Jordan full of the Holy Spirit and was led by the Spirit into the desert, where He was tempted by the devil for forty days. In all that time He ate nothing, so that He was hungry when it was over.

Devil: If you are God's son, order this stone to turn into bread.

Jesus: The scripture says, "Man cannot live on bread alone."

Choir: Then the devil took Him up and showed Him in a second all the kingdoms of the world.

Devil: I will give you all this power, and all this wealth. It was handed over to me and I can give it to anyone I choose. All this will be yours, then, if you will kneel down before me.

Jesus: The scripture says, "Worship the Lord your God and serve only Him!"

Choir: Then the devil took Him to Jerusalem and set Him on the highest point of the temple.

Devil: If you are God's son, throw yourself down from here. For the scripture says, "God will order his angels to take good care of you." It also says, "They will hold you up with their hands so that not even your feet will be hurt on the stones."

Jesus: The scripture says, "You must not put the Lord your God to the test."

Choir: When the devil finished tempting Jesus in every way, he left Him for a while.

Luke 15:11-32
Drama For Verse-Speaking Choir

Choir:	Hear this story as told by Jesus of Nazareth in Luke, chapter 15 (from the Good News Bible).
Younger Son:	Father, give me my share of the property now.
Choir:	So the man divided his property between his two sons. After a few days the younger son sold his part of the property and left home with the money.He went to a country far away, where he wasted his money in reckless living. After he had spent every thing he had, a severe famine spread over that country. So he went to work for a farmer who sent him out to take care of the pigs. He wished he could fill himself with the bean pods the pigs ate, but no one gave him anything to eat. At last he came to his senses.
Younger Son:	All my father's hired workers have more than they can eat, and here I am about to starve. I'll get up and go to my father and say, "Father, I have sinned against God and against you. I am no longer fit to be called your son; treat me as one of your hired workers."
Choir:	So he got up and started back to his father. But while he was still a long way from home, his father saw him and his heart was filled with pity. The father ran to his son and threw his arms around him and kissed him.
Younger Son:	Father, I have sinned against God and against you. I am no longer fit to be called your son.

Father: Servants! Hurry! Bring the best robe and put it on my son. Put a ring on his finger and shoes on his feet. Then go get the prize calf and kill it for a great feast! This son of mine was once dead, but now he is alive! He once was lost, but now he has been found.

Choir: And so the feasting began. The older son, in the meantime, was out in the field. On his way back, when he came close to the house, he heard the music and dancing. He called to one of the servants.

Older Son: What's going on here?

Servant: Your brother has come back home safe and sound and your father had the prize calf killed for a great feast.

Choir: The older brother was so angry that he would not go into the house; so his father came out to him.

Father: Son, come in and join us in the celebration. Your brother has come home.

Older Son: Look, all these years I have worked like a slave for you, and I never disobeyed your orders. What have you given me? Not even a goat for me to have a feast with my friends! But this son of yours wasted all your property with women of the street, and when he comes back home you kill the prize calf for him!

Father: My son, you are always here with me and everything I have is yours. But we need to have a feast and be happy, because your brother was dead, but now he is alive! He was lost, but now he has been found!

The Mustard Seed

Matthew 13:31, 32

Mary Isabelle Hock

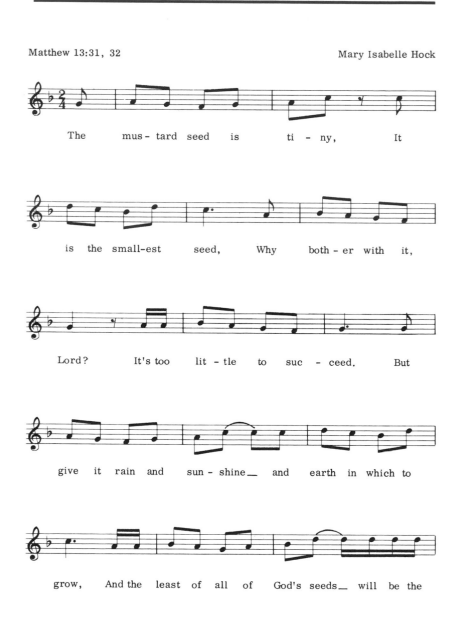

The mus - tard seed is ti - ny, It

is the small-est seed, Why both - er with it,

Lord? It's too lit - tle to suc - ceed. But

give it rain and sun - shine__ and earth in which to

grow, And the least of all of God's seeds__ will be the

great - est tree you know! Just see it grow - ing

tall - er, The birds find shel - ter there. It's

part of God's cre - a - tion, It blos-soms eve - ry

where. It's as our good Lord told us___ the

King-dom of Heav - en sto - ry;___ though we are small and

hum - ble___ we too can grow in His glo - ry!___

The Mustard Seed
Ideas for use

Use —

1. as a cherub choir song.

2. for creative play. The children can be seeds scattered around the room in low position growing very slowly. A few children will move as birds, rain, and sunshine.

3. as interpretative movement. A few dancers can be positioned at the low level to represent the growing seeds. Three dancers with flowing scarves at different levels can be moving at various times. One could begin at the beginning of the song, one at "rain," and one at "birds." One verse of the song could be repeated and all the dancers including the seeds praise God in movement.

Apostles Creed I

Mary Isabelle Hock

I be-lieve in God the Fa - ther____ Al -

might - y, Mak - er of heav - en and earth; and in

Je - sus Christ His on - ly Son, ____ our Lord. Who was con -

ceived by the Ho - ly Spir - it, ____ born of the Vir - gin

Mar - y, ____ suf-fered un - der Pon - tius Pi - late, ___ was

cru - ci-fied, dead, and bur - ied; ___ the third day

He rose from the dead; He as - cend - ed in - to

heav-en___ and sit toth at the right hand___ of God, the

Fa - ther___ Al - might - y; From thence He shall

come to judge the quick and the dead. I be -

lieve in the Ho - ly Spir - it___ the ho - ly cath - olic

church, the com - mun - ion of___ saints, the for -

give-ness of___ sins, the res - ur - rec - tion of the___

bod - y___ and the life ev-er-last - ing. A - men.

Apostles Creed II

Mary Isabelle Hock

I be-lieve in God, the Fa - ther___ Al -
might - y, Cre - a - tor of heav - en and earth; and in
Je - sus Christ His on - ly Son, _____ our Lord,
Who was con-ceived by the pow'r of the Ho - ly Spir -it, __
Born of the Vir- gin Mar - y, Suf-fered un-der Pon -tius
Pi - late, __ was cru - ci -fied, died and was
bur-ied; He de-scend- ed in - to hell. On the third day

The Apostles'Creed set to music is very helpful in memorizing and remembering the Creed.
It is also a beautiful setting for interpretative movement.

He rose __ a -gain. He as - cend -ed in - to

heav - en __ and is seat-ed at the right hand __ of the Fa ——

ther. __ He will come __ a - gain to judge the liv - ing __

__ and the dead. I be - lieve in the Ho - ly

Spir - it __ the ho - ly cath-olic church, the com-

mun - ion of __ saints, the for - give-ness of __

sins, the res-ur - rec -tion of the __ bod - y __ and the

life ev - er - last - ing. A - men.

Praising Him In Service
Visiting the Confined

---

1. Pray for God's guidance; you are his representative.

2. Remember the confined is a person; focus on his needs, not on yourself.

3. Have permission or implied consent of patient to be present.

4. Be aware of person's right to maintain a distance in the relationship.

5. Listen, listen! Decode message, catch feelings to understand!
   a. Concentrate on verbal and non-verbal behavior and what the patient is feeling no matter what he is saying. (If he prefers silence, be silent and caring.)
   b. Let patient ventilate emotions of anger, fear, guilt, despair, etc.
   c. Be yourself, be warm and friendly, touching if appropriate.

6. Give undivided attention to demonstrate caring and desire to help.
   a. Show empathy.
   b. Silence is an excellent response.
   c. Remember to refrain from giving advice, or amplifying patient's feelings, or putting down his fear, or promising healing.
   d. A scripture or a short prayer may be helpful.

7. Discuss spiritual and family concerns, not medical concerns.

8. Ask questions about past events and progress toward the present when a patient seems confused, as early life experiences are more clear in the memory of the elderly.

9. Leave cards with the church's name, address, and telephone number with patients and shut-ins.
a. Relatives will be aware that the patient had a visitor from the church when the patient is unable to communicate.
b. The visitor may write his own name and telephone number on the card if he feels the patient may need to call him.
c. The visitor may write a message on the card to leave by a sleeping patient.
d. The card by the telephone assures a shut-in that he can contact his church or his visitor when he is lonely or has an emergency.

10. Select literature or tapes from the church to take to shut-ins.

11. Visit in teams if possible when shut-in is of opposite sex.

12. Remember that relating information about the patient is a criminal invasion of privacy and is grounds for a lawsuit.

I Rest, Lord In Thee

Meditation

Mary Isabelle Hock

I am qui - et, I am peace - ful. I ___

rest, Lord, in Thee. I am filled with Thy

Pres -ence. I am bliss - ful, I am free.

CHRISTIAN HOME

God Bless Mothers

Mary Isabelle Hock

We thank You, God for flow - ers, For friends and toys and play. We thank You most for moth - ers, ___ God, bless them all to - day.

A Tribute To Mothers

Traditional Gaelic Melody
"Morning Has Broken"

Dear God we thank You for all our moth - ers. You've made them lov - ing in eve - ry way. They are so pa - tient, and un - der - stand - ing. Lord, give Your bless - ings on moth - ers to - day.

After the children sing the verse, they can move with brightly colored streamers or scarves and then repeat the verse.

Mother's Day—Father's Day

I love you, Mother (Father)
And thank you too,
For all the loving
Things you do.

I blow you a kiss *(action, sound)*
To show you I care.
And give you a hug *(action, "mm" sound)*
My love to share.

You're the best mother (father)
And that's why I say,
I love you so much
On this Mother's (Father's) Day!

(Kiss and hug with actions and sounds)

A Prayer For Fathers

Bless all fathers, Lord, we pray,
Keep them safe by night and day.
Give them strength to do your will,
And their needs, dear Lord, fulfill.
Bless them with your peace and love
With heavenly wisdom from above.
Bless them all each day this year
With your presence ever near.

Shower their families with blessings too,
With an abundance of joy in You.
Help them pray and know You, Lord,
O bind them together in one accord.
Show the fathers their rightful place;
Give them guidance, Lord, and grace.
Bless the fathers, Lord, we pray;
Fill them with Christ and your word each day.
Bless each father and family
With love, O Lord, from Thee.

Lyrics by Mary Isabelle Hock
Music by May H. Brahe, "Bless This House"

Hats Off To Mothers And Fathers
Write Your Own Choral Reading

1. All students learn the following verse:
    Happy Mother's (Father's) Day,
    We love you, Mother (Father) dear;
    May God richly bless you
    Today and all the year.
    We take our hats off to you
    To show our thanks for all you do.
    (All take hats off.)

2. Any number of people may write a line of appreciation
    of a parent and these statements can be done as solos.

3. All put hats on.

4. The group then repeats the original verse and takes their
    hats off again.

5. Hats can be brought from home, or the students can
    create their own headgear.

Example on next page

Hats Off To Mothers

Choral reading written and presented by a fourth grade class wearing hats

All: Happy Mother's Day,
               We love you, Mother dear;
               May God richly bless you
               Today and all the year.
               We take our hats off to you,*
               To show our thanks for all you do.

Solo 1:   Mothers, we thank you for helping us do
               our homework.

Solo 2:   For buying us presents and new clothes,

Solo 3:   For making us do chores and giving us an
               allowance.

Solo 4:   For working hard and cleaning the house,

Solo 5:   For all your chauffeuring and doing the
               laundry,

Solo 6:   For tucking us in bed and comforting us,

Solo 7:   For taking us on vacations and sharing
               your love with us.

All: Happy Mother's Day,**
               We love you, Mother dear;
               May God richly bless you
               Today and all the year.
               We take our hats off to you,*
               To show our thanks for all you do.

*Take hats off **Put hats on

Children's Song Of Praise

Song	Movement
	Children stand with arms at sides.
Group A: Father, we love You.	*Raise both arms up high, and hold.*
Group B: Father, we praise You.	*Raise both arms up high, hold.*
Group A: Hear us your children.	*Bring both arms down, hands come together in front*
Group B: Hear us we pray.	*at waist level with palms up, hold.*
Group A: Father, we love You.	*Raise arms high, hold.*
Group B: Father, we praise You.	*Raise arms high.*
All: Thank You for your blessings	*Bring both arms down and on "blessings" cross arms on chest,*
On your children today.	*then both arms go down at sides.*
Let us clap.	*On "clap" clap hands.*
Let us dance.	*Hands on hips, on "dance" do one slide step to the right.*
Let us sing with joy!	*Hands still on hips, do one slide step to left on "sing." On "joy" raise arms high.*
Thank You for your blessings	*Bring both arms down and on "blessings" cross arms on chest,*
On each girl and boy.	*then both arms go down to the sides.*

Children's Song Of Praise

Mary Isabelle Hock

Fa - ther, we love You.   Fa - ther, we praise You.

Hear   us Your chil - dren,   Hear   us   we pray.

Fa - ther, we   love   You.   Fa - ther, we praise You.

Thank You for Your bless-ings on Your   chil - dren to -day. Let us

clap,   let us dance! Let   us   sing   with   joy!

Thank You for Your bless-ings on each   girl   and   boy.

King's Kids

Mary Isabelle Hock

All praise to You, Je - sus, ___ Joy - ful - ly we

sing, We give You all the glo - ry, ___ We are

Kids of the King. Praise, praise, Je - sus ___

Joy, joy we sing. Glo - ry, glo - ry

glo - ry, ___ We are Kids of the King, We are

Group 1

Kids of the King! All praise to You, Je - sus ___

Blessing All A-Round

Mary Isabelle Hock

Praise the Fa - ther, Praise the Son,
Bless our house - holds, Lord, we pray

Praise to the Spir - it Who makes us __ one.
Love, joy and peace be on fam -'lies to - day.

A Dedication Of A Home

(As people enter, each one receives a cross made from wood or macrame, yarn, cardboard, beads, bread dough — be creative!)

Host: Welcome to our (new) home. Grace and peace to you from God our father, and from the Lord Jesus Christ.

(All gather in the main room and host lights a scented candle.)

Host: Let us light this candle as a symbol of the light of Christ shining in this home.

Prayer: Dear Father, we are gathered here to dedicate this house to You that it may become a home enriched with your divine blessings. Father, bless all who live in this home with love, understanding and patience that they may prosper in all ways. May the Holy Spirit fill each person with peace and joy that loving relationships will grow and flourish under your divine guidance. May the hospitality be overflowing and uplifting to all who enter this home. And, Father, we pray for your divine blessings on this home that all evil will PASS OVER, and only good shall come to this dwelling, to this property, and to your people. We pray this in the name of Jesus who taught us to pray.

(All pray together the Lord's Prayer.)

Scripture:	Proverbs 24:3-4: "By wisdom a house is built..." Matthew 7:24,25: "Founded on the rock..." Ephesians 2:19-22: "Christ...the corner stone..." Psalm 23: (*All read together or a leader may say a phrase and all repeat it.*)

(All sing and walk through all the rooms holding their crosses to signify an act of cleansing and purification, with the host carrying the lighted scented candle symbolizing the light and fragrance of Jesus Christ being spread throughout the home.)

Song:	**(Tune, "Blest be the tie that binds")**

Lord, bless this house today,
May it be wholly thine.
And may your love and joy and peace
Fill each room with blessings divine.

Benediction:	Now may the Lord of peace Himself give you peace at all times in all ways. The Lord be with you all.

(II Thessolonians 3:16 RSV)

(A lunch or communion may be served while all sing "Let us break bread together.")